TO KNOW WE ARE LIVING

TO KNOW
WE ARE LIVING

POEMS BY

Miriam Levine

DHP

DECATUR HOUSE PRESS
WASHINGTON, D. C.

FIRST EDITION

Grateful acknowledgment is made to the following publications in which some of these poems have appeared: *Big Moon, Choomia, Ironwood, The Lamp in the Spine, Mother Jones, Our Poets' Workshop, Out of the Ashes, Poetry Now, Second Coming, The Tufts Review.*

"Evelyn" and "Need" appeared in a chapbook, *Friends Dreaming,* copyright 1974 by Ironwood Press.

LIBRARY OF CONGRESS CATALOGING
IN PUBLICATION DATA

Levine, Miriam
    To know we are living.

    I. Title.
√ PS3562.E898T6   811'.5'4   76-204
ISBN 0-916276-01-5

Decatur House Press, Ltd.
2122 Decatur Place, NW
Washington, D.C.   20008

CONTENTS

Foreword by Denise Levertov

PART I: I DREAMT THAT CERTAIN WOMEN

PART II: SEEING THINGS

PART III: BROTHER, LISTEN

PART IV: BEAUTIFUL SUNDAY

PART V: THE BLINDMAN AND THE ROSE

FOREWORD

Miriam Levine's name is one which has habitually come to my mind when, in the last couple of years, I have been asked the perennial question, *Who are the interesting younger and lesser-known poets?*

Her's is—at this stage of her life as a writer—a somewhat introverted poetry, drawing heavily on dream and fantasy; while much of what interests me in other younger writers deals more directly with the external world. But what I admire in her work is the evident authenticity and intensity of her images, and the intelligence and literacy with which she discovers the vivid words of her experience. *Feast,* one of the poems in this collection that I like best, well exemplifies both her achievement and her potential: it makes us share a kind of terror, while the economy and firmness with which it is wrought give pleasure; thus the poem provides, on a small scale, something of the experience of catharsis.

Denise Levertov
September 1975

FOR MY MOTHER AND FATHER

PART I

I DREAMT THAT CERTAIN WOMEN

I DREAMT THAT CERTAIN WOMEN

I dreamt that certain women
were sending me letters:

Dear Child
Where have you been so long?
Why not join us?

The one with jet beads
And the one with the heart of flowers
and the voice humming like a wasp in my dreams

Doves cooing in the pink air of morning
The clear notes of reason
and the bitter drones of survivors
ready for anything—

stumbling, uncombed
I find paper in the dark
and a pen
        to answer . . .

EVELYN

Because I am back in Passaic
near the river
on the low streets

because I am trying to sleep
in my mother's house
I feel differently

behind the thin door
behind the thin walls
the convulsion visceral
stabbing in the guts

a woman alone
walking through Roxbury

a woman alone
carrying gasoline

a woman alone
carrying what they will use
to kill you

my fear
our fear
to be the victim

to be surrounded
to be caught powerless

to be made to pour gasoline
over yourself

to dig your own grave
to participate
to help your murderers
knot the rope that hangs you
to walk into the showers
into the train

to be forced to sit
surrounded and cursed

to be made to pour gasoline over your head

to know as you do this
that you will burn
that they will touch the match and watch

to know that no one will save you
no brother will save you

to be made to help the enemy kill you
to be the victim completely

Evelyn
they back off and run

and still you walk burning
walk slowly along the street
alone, a wonder burning

a man looks up
walks from behind the counter
hands outstretched
stopped outside the circle of flame

no one can cross the space around you

you are speaking calmly
hair still burning, face burned black

the victim and not the victim
speaking calmly

You had seen
You had been made to help them kill you

NEED

> She needed someone to smooth her blouse,
> to smooth away the awkwardness from her shoulders.
> —*His Poem*

1. She needed to have
her hands and feet
tied to the hooves

skin peeled off in one piece
like a roasted pepper

ears flattened
with sewing tacks

nose broken and straightened

she needed to be bitten
by the snake

scraped out
like an egg

eaten with salt
and a small silver spoon

If he would wrap his hands
around the tendrils of her hair
and pull, she would know
how much she existed

2. She needed
someone to trace
the blue veins
on her inner arms

paint her belly with slime
dye the bottoms of her feet
bright purple

touch
until she could feel
each tooth in her mouth

each bone and the web

3. She needed a son
who sucked milk
and did not dream of blood

the slippery handle, the damp sheath

who did not see a nest of snakes
growing in her head

polyp to crush
soft egg to crack and suck

4. She needed to die
to put her head down
on her folded arms

and sleep the long sleep
of obliteration

5. She needed to kill him
probing the circuits of his brain
unwinding coils

bathing his smile in milk
winding him in ribbons
for the long journey

Carefully, she folded
the map without names

pushed him
out of the car
into the desert
one match taped to his hand

RED VENUS

She stands on the stone
where he puts her

A buried seed
without eyes

A root, a stone
pocked and swollen

pulled down
to her own belly

round and high as the moon

deep slit
naked and open

Sewn into her own walls
She cannot move

Over and over
the tight red stone

They rub
They rub themselves alive

MEN CRYING

He cries in my dreams
a close-up shot
I reach out and feel his tears

He cries in his sleep
dreaming of walls
and towers, the ax and the rope

He rolls on the floor
knees to his head
sobbing and begging
for his wife

He cries when he leaves her
grey and shrunken
in the white bed

He cries when she dies
pouring water
cupful after cupful
over his hands

He cries in the docket
his palms sweat
in the visitors' room

He screams when he sticks
the scarab pin into his eyes

when the net is thrown
and the knife slips in

He sobs when they beat him
he faints when he is burned

He weeps when the nurse
touches his forehead

He barks
dry hard sobs
holding back
when she hits him

WRITING AT NIGHT

Writing at night
frightens me
the sound of pipes
water slowly trickling
dark house
dark kitchen
I can hear my own blood
strange what you become
mornings saved for writing
desk at the window
where the sun comes in
the heart easy
not like this
night in winter
frozen over
the trees are frozen

Nights of the past
city nights awake
in furnished rooms
smelling of paint
dry heat blossoms
windows facing windows
suns going down in windows
the night I saw a man
escaping across the roof
the cellar room
roaches coming out
when I turned off the light
knowing how they crawled
around the stove

one step between bed and desk
three new books pen and paper
alone and awake
                    for long nights
waking in the night
finding the light on
books slipped to the floor
waking and starting again
writing or taking up the book
where I left off
falling back
                    taking up the dream
nights strung out .
breakfasts in cafeterias
a door between gritty lions

First the child falls asleep
then he falls asleep
and if I'm awake
they pull me after them
I walk in and out of their rooms
watching them sleep
watching them smile in their sleep

A car whines on the ice
the clocks hum
the sleepers pull me after them
come lie with us
sleep and forget
in the morning
I am always in his arms

They pull me in
sleep when I sleep
be warm when I am warm
and I've been following
unresisting
giving up my white nights
my night fears
sound of houses
my own blood
myself, alone and awake

TO THE MUSE

And in that emptiness we both share
the same command to ride away is given.
      —*Marina Tsvetayeva*

In the blue shadow
in the cabin in the snow
the poet waits for you
he is sure he knows your name
Mother of Life, Mother of Death
Mother of Stone, Mother of Joy
Yakshī snake-hipped dancing
your rosy mouth against his ear
your hand over his hand
he swells in your eyes
in your full-lipped smile

I've waited for my father
his white ship
shining like porcelain
his colors black and purple
I freeze when he touches my arm
I wander in his dark house

I become my own mother
my sisters' mother
my mother's mother

you become mine!
I am talking to you, Anna
to you, Marina
I take the milky drop
the kernel dripping blue sugar
my own muse
my own moon

Now if I am starving
I starve myself

Now if I ride away
I ride away from myself

No more commands will be given

MERMAN

This has been
a month of visits
from the sulphur mines
the vineyard, the moon

he steps through
cold American appliances
white enameled surfaces
the way Cocteau's Orpheus
steps through mirrors
out of green water
clean and inhuman

his white collar is starched
sharp as a razor
his sex bulges
under a soft camel hair coat

I get what I never asked for
dirt and water
fire and water

I learn to love what I hate
to be excited by aliens
his green Atlantic eyes
his dead white skin

he comes for fire and dirt—
cold kisses   cold sperm
without knowing it
I've summoned my opposite

he's here to show me
the end of simplicity
the watery dream
treacherous and perverse

because it comes   unasked for
because it comes   cold and repellent

BOY MUSE

I am tired of old men
I am sick of fathers
I desert my mentors
forget their lessons
despise their wisdom
become thoughtless
stare into space
haunt windows

and the boy comes
swaying against me
dolphin breathing
wine-stained mouth
against my ear

he leans back smiling
his long dark hair damp and tangled

a boy who is like a girl

my fingers curl
inside his warm hand
his voice laps like water
when my mouth moves
I feel his lips

I take the old man
the old father
his cold body
into my body
he warms up slowly
when I love the boy
the old man is quiet

I drink for hours
forgetting everything I knew
watching his slanting eyes
his hot face flushed with wine
I become
a woman who is like a man

THE SOUL OF A WOMAN, THE EYES OF A MAN

If I came to you
Medusa-haired
the body of a woman
the head of a bird

the body of a bird
the head of a woman
the swooning, open-mouthed
face of love

you would look over your shoulder
for the enemy

Feeling your hair
grow through your skin
the chemical vertigo
of sickness and love
I try to find a soul

Your dreams give me nothing

Your eyes turn hyacinth
purple flower, purple stone

In your body
in your silver blood
your jeweled face

the mocking god, smiling

at the hunger of the wolf
for the blue robe, the moth

PART II

SEEING THINGS

SEEING THINGS

i

> A honey bee by stinging me
> Did stop my mortal breath
> —*Tombstone Inscription*

> *Abeja blanca zumbas, ebria de miel, en mi alma*
> —*Neruda*

Driving off the green hill
waves of heat
shimmer up blinding
no sun
only the red honeycomb eye
through the half-moon window
Richard Widmark's hatchet face
stretched tight burn
amber: out of the glare
slowly a soft face grows in the blur

Remember in the city
looking from the kitchen window
we saw a face
moon haunted white mask
cycladic in the weeds
after weeks you had to see
it was a plastic bleach jug
the eyes we saw were shadows
in the hollows
on the sides of the handle

Into cool shade
maples touching overhead
slowing to second
a dog's black head
on a man's torso
hands at his side
dog, bird, Amun-Ra

Bees buzzing
a string of beads quivering
along the length of yellow tassels
fringe hanging down
bat-grey wings folded back

the child laughs soft mouthed
green caterpillar tongue licking ices

your shoulder stained ochre
streaked claw marks
tiger   lily
                pollen

bees heavy in the phlox
messenger stripes

I believe what I see

ii

> I love the whale . . .
> —*Bly*

Out on the curve
silver backing toward me
slow bird dancing
heat rippling lightning sky
three eyed tail
bullet blue flame
the whale is dead!
two men ride like insects in his brain
down the black strip into the blue

In the glass tower
on the concrete rim
cool aluminum
nothing grows
only our cells
inside the machine
sleek shark palisades

The girl points her white gloved finger
the killer whale surges up
straight as a rocket tail beating
lunging   touches the small red ball

This is the package   This is the present
For the first time   I enter

iii

There is a Moment in each Day that Satan cannot find
—Blake

Listening to María la de Triana
chalk house against the red sky
Granada, halved pomegranate
suns open to suns on the Sierra Nevada
a black dog passes
in the late afternoon
I rock in a chair next to the window
he comes in carrying a ball of string
we unwind it
looping a chain eye into eye

What would happen if she
walked between the houses
smelling of myrtle and jasmin
into the song and disappeared?

iv

During the Watergate Hearings, July 1973

> But in the room of the banished poet
> Fear and the Muse stand watch by turn . . .
> —*Akhmatova*

Anna's book slips from my hand
the lamp is still on
light on the quilt
I am the fugitive
in fantasy planning
bit by bit Robinson Crusoe
an island off the coast of Maine
granite and sea lavender
weather beaten silver shingles
an abandoned house
green to the door
a lobster smack bought in secret
through agents—can you do that?
pushing off at night
holding our children
our friends' children

Night by night
I take it up again
the harbor must be hidden
no one must see us leave
is there a place like that
dark to all human eyes?
and the books and paper
medicine and bandages
seeds and wool, needles
pick and shovel, plow
we are the horses
strapped in the harness
two goats tethered in the ark
are there empty islands?
the essentials of our cargo grow heavy

On the third night
I consider the Franks
listening behind the dummy door
human inside the hole
people on the narrow bridges
light on the houses
while they waited—No

I build and build in my mind
my obsession is satisfying
I reach the winter wood stove
the smoke!
would they bother?
Who are they?
I'm not sure
but now we need them
to stay hidden
we are the hiders
writing with cold fingers
we need to hear "the clangor
of the Black Marias" to know we are living

I go to bed early
I want to get back so badly
it comes, the enormity of it
we bring flour and sugar
then we learn to make them
wrapped in a white sheet
Bill smokes the bees quiet
growing wheat, dandelion wine
for the winter
we start early before the winter
beginning . . . I can't start from the beginning!

When the engine dies
we travel at night
on country roads
house to house *
underground—No

Start now!
choose to go back
before the fantasy
walk around the walls
watch the faces of toll collectors

PART III

BROTHER, LISTEN

SWIMMER

There is no heaven for Dante
without Beatrice,
no hell without Latini—

smoking in the shadow of the porch
I watch you stroke face down
in greenish water

sun catching your arms as you lift them

again and again

rising glistening
above the murky drag

coming out

so near

YEARS

1. Jungle

Count the years
taste them
tighten your fist
press your knuckles
against your mouth
taste the bony ridge

Insects
filing across the dry
places of the marsh

You and I
in the same line
step by step
across the plank

sweat beads on your forehead
like sand scars
the rock sweats

patterns of shadow
play along your shoulders

and I lose you

measure the rope and the noose
notice the regularity of the pump
the dry circle
worn in the grass

another man
drinks in the mountains

pictures hum behind my eyes

the peasant and the soldier
squatting in the clearing

We are talking
lying again:

"Are trees masculine or feminine?"
"It depends on the weather."

2. The Wolf and the Fish

You advance
I withdraw

I advance
You withdraw

endlessly!

In the heat
the blow torch
the yellow flame
that curls around our ears

You choose water
I choose fur:

In our next life
we are extinct

Your elusive body
cools in the shallows

You tell me
I like to burn!
I like to burn

3. Fever

When I called
in my sleep
she came

touched my forehead
with her cool hand

bathed me
brushed back my damp hair

When I opened my eyes
she was waiting

*

I press the button
and you drink

For the first time
I ask

you stop counting
your fist loosens

I put my lips
against your wrist

Darting against my hair
you save me from burning

NOW EVERYTHING IS REAL

Now everything is real

A single horse
grazes in a field

we go riding

Smiling
intimate of this place

between the rocks
shapes of the mother and father
pillars of salt

each striation
burned by the wind

You find water

In the dryness
In the rust

*

The black shape
slices through water

You swim toward it

there is no thought
just the pure intention
of your body

Not in the belly of the whale
But riding the whale!

Its hard skin
the soft hole

Foetal
small legs gripping

you ride in the instant of his quiet
the beast who is alien and like you

His tail beats and slashes:
the wind and the razor—

When you tell me
I see

Everything

ONLY THE DEATH

Only the death
you are preparing
is pure

your body
trained for extremity
the knife, the fall

diving into black water
blind fish nose against your mask—
what is this thing, this man?

You take the stone in your teeth
and the mountain

riding the taut wire
making it sing

a motion
which keeps you alive

a motion
which brings you closer

In the early morning
is your equilibrium
your space
the light blue and rose

Take this rest
the flower of mould and dirt

Blackness
Nada
the worms do not sing

So perfect
without sound

So pure
in its absence
without breathing

Tell me you give up
this lover who is not a lover

This perfection!
This nothing!
This blackness!

BROTHER, LISTEN

Brother, listen
to the thunder
the others are sleeping
their hands soft and open

There is no coil
waiting to spring

The light inside the room
is the light outside the room

The walls are throbbing
the bells, the horn

The air inside the room
is the air outside the room

We breathe it
the distances close

In half-light
In shadow

in the tongue of the bell
in the throat of the horn

things happen

We are not meant to be pure

MIRAGE

I've gone through the door
into the damp
into the room without birds
the room without food
without light

The trophies
like a skyline
which you deny
and live with

Instead of sleep
Instead of coolness

You give me a thing
which seems like food
a drink which seems wet

A mirage!

You give me
a thing
that seems like rest

A death
that seems like life

I eat and starve

I RENOUNCE

I renounce
your lying eyes
and your mouth of snow

there is no difference
between the mask of fire
and the mask of ice

I send you back
to the slaughtered pig
to the bull and the cock
who must die

To the yellow sun
and the red sun

I turn you in
to the authorities
whose medals you wear

to the private army
who love you

Go back
to the ball with no center
to the tree without roots

Taste it!

this world
which brings you
to one place

GEOGRAPHY

Three hundred windows
above the plains of humiliation

I who loved dirt
who prayed at crossroads

balance on a rail

One flicker
could hurl me down
through a sky of eagles
among a thousand white burros
into spikes of tenacity

the pitted road
where you ride

slumped in the back seat
guts running with shit

Taken!
Driven!
by women:
María de los Angeles
her friend and the child

Cool lady of afternoons,
at the edge of dust
the crowd of ragged children
swarming through mud and cotton,
I admit to hands and faces
rising, unfurling under the lifted hood

beseeching, possessed
singing to your helplessness:
Do something! you're a man, a man, a man

and the fourth watching
counting the days

and the other
who isn't born
who curls, moving her lips

STRANGERS

For J. L.

We walked there together
I had prepared
We were both excited
He thought he was taking me
We were taking each other
He led me to the clearing
Because he knew the way
The large rock
Had a top like a table
I lay across it
He stood with his face in shadow
He was no more my husband
Than I was his wife

PART IV

BEAUTIFUL SUNDAY

FLOWER

Compelled
by an urgency
of space

I pick the flower
to begin

a room
a road

the sweep of an arm
drawing you in to
the tip of powder

I throw

Where there was nothing!
It hits

Flames
with honey

A sudden swarm
beats   turning

lashing its soft fire

THERE ARE SOFT THINGS

There are soft things
falling through doorways
like flowers

He moves

In the light of our arms
he moves closer

Black moth
through webs
through draughts
sucked under stones into coolness

his wayward flickering movement

Can you believe!
how he goes

Feeding against us
in the purple mouth
of the basket of flowers
in the petals' soft skin

Can you believe!
how softly he beats
his heavy wings

brushing the blue
streak of sulphur

the pungent, fermenting
darkness around us

MOTH, FIRE, MUD

The way spirit lives
in the witch's doll
you inhabit my dream

in the segmented bodies
of marionettes
crumpled, unstrung

until my fingers spread
your silken sleeves
the way a woman separates
a skein of wool
lifting you from scarlet rustlings

tap   tap   go   your
shiny black feet

Your sleeves are wings
velvet rainbows
dew transparencies of the moth

Now your mad eyes
are printed on their wings

What holds you to this earth?
Your house is burning
its furniture cracking
falling through the floors

the roof is caught
the chimney falling

Your children are waking in the flames
You calmly ask me for a favor

Softly   softly
go your silken wings

too late to plant your feet in mud

I AM AFRAID

> Things cannot know us.
> —*Roethke*

I am afraid
of the day of illusion

pale coffee-colored slugs
lace-mouthed limpets
drained of light

lichens, chalk-green and orange

of being able
to define

the point where light
splits open
to a black seed

We pour our eyes into things
What comes back?

Here is scarlet
Here is blue

Here is rust and ochre
colors like blood and food

Those days that glow—
the beginnings of fear

forming in shadows
the corners

It is the other side
dullness without lustre—

The raven's wing
has a bluish sheen

Black rainbow!
I fix my eyes

DO YOU?

What can you take
from the mycologist
who wanders into your picnic
with the wrong mushrooms?

What do you find in the sea?

Sweet plump pearl of oyster
The fish with a clock in its belly
A hermit crab with its death-hold on the clam

The yellow luminous dial
from the tongued brush of the worker
shines through the bones
the hour hand jumps at the tick

Do you want to believe?

Go out after dinner
to walk the beach
swinging back and forth over water

searching the phosphorescent gleamings
in the windrows of seaweed
that pulse in your hand

taking life from your life
cool bluish heat washed up

Can you bake them in a pie?
Can you put them in your hair?

The red moon rises and swells
regular as an eye of coral
and the long white line of surf

Put them on your table
live in their constancy
See how far they take you

BEAUTIFUL SUNDAY

The streets are empty as a jar

I could begin an important job
something that would give me satisfaction

but I wander to the windows
one after another
all morning long

Their brightness oppresses me

The words of one sentence
shake against each other
the first forgotten
the last trailing off

We should have gone to the orchard today
instead of yesterday in the rain

I can't get started
reminding myself of too many things
feeling the presence of others
which isn't their fault

I could walk, taking a book
or leaving that behind
have my coffee outside in the sun

but somehow things lack savor
although I'm not despairing

Beautiful   Beautiful   Sunday!

and I can do nothing

the day has already been taken

It's been waiting
but I don't want to lie down

EVIDENCE

I lived
in this room
with blue sills

Walked
in a reef of yellow light

Twice
my child looked at me
with fear in his eyes

I've gnawed the bone
and sucked the marrow

If the workers of Strunino
don't come to my window
with money to save me

Won't you hear my voice
in the swirl of black ink
you hold to your ear?

THINGS BEGIN

Things begin
and we don't know
where they will end

Waking in the dark
the first line comes
like a hand at my throat
a constriction, a caress

That yellow window
swells like the moon
and I'm on my way

Records are made
for the light of morning
when I return to the beginning
which gripped me

like remembered voices
of the dead
coming up through lilacs
with their urgent whispers of smoke

So it is with you:
The first line set down

Indelibly

Seeded

Who knows
how far it will take us . . .

PART V

THE BLINDMAN AND THE ROSE

IN THE GLASS

Walking in the cool world to see them.
The porch, light swirling
in its frame like a rain cloud,
curves around the wooden tower.
Everything goes black in the shade
stepping off the beach in Maine.
The children are resting on green cots
and the patients are sleeping
and the nurse wheels on metal carts
trays of milk equally measured in glasses
and the floors are waxed smooth and yellow
and the eggman's wife sweeps the porch after lunch
and the maids polish the silver
in the houses of the wool merchants
I passed on my way to the library.
Under the splintering floor of my room
heated all summer by the boiler,
springs bubbled in the coal bins;
water dripped from intimate things
in the courtyard outside my window;
flies, green-gold and black, rubbed
their legs against the screen—
before I can ring, he's standing
in the high green doorway watching;
his silk pops open like a parachute;
over its black wings the sun shower's
sulfurous clouds, blue and gunmetal,
drip gold on the grass sunken below the road,
as if the road we walk on were a dam in Holland.
I look for my mother's face in the window;
the wind blows the razor-pleated gauze
into the blackness while my father talks:
"So different from before." I watch
him growing smaller and smaller, a dot,
walking back to wake her and the thick
glass closes in my sleep like an eye.

FEAST

This is how:
the flicker of an eyelid
across the sun
quick chill

seasons of hot afternoons
the steady pulse
of the wing
in your wrist
felt but not seen

the longest afternoon deepens
encroaching

the grass is high and cool
even the legs of the table
are sunk in grass

The king cuts the pie
The queen eats

The children of the queen
lick their fingers clean
tender crust melts
on their soft pink tongues
as they fall asleep

Now through the broken crust
wet and black with sugar
the birds poke their scrawny
new-born heads
all beak and goggle eye

slowly as paper
they dry to gloss

Once seen
            they will feast and feast
the lords of everything

WHAT I WAS AFRAID OF HAS HAPPENED

For D. T.

When I said no
I was immediately sorry

You see, I'm against the wall
or the wall is in front of me

Watching your yellow smock
at nine o'clock in the morning
your folded hands which suddenly open
is not going to help me

I'm coming up against it
I need to breathe deeply
It's not easy

Something is waiting for me

and I can't open it like a letter
and read the sharp print leaping out

I've written the large N and the large O
in my own hand without trembling or shaking

But a simple no spoken to you
touches the lock in the gate

Behind the wall
a wild child runs and dances
her dress is white
her face is willful and abandoned

She pleases herself
and makes no explanations

Blond as I am dark
She dances!
and defies her mother

MIRACLE

I was alone in the house
when the lights went out

There was no one upstairs
There was no one downstairs

I looked out the window
the street was dark

I found a bag of candles
stuck in a drawer

and when the blaze was kindled
I drew out my cloth

When everything was polished
shiny as a bone

I made a pot of coffee
to welcome you home

The cracks from my hammer are hidden
and the shadows are warm as a pillow

Mother, Mother
come into your kitchen

The street is dark
the school is gone

I'm here in my smock
with my hair tied back

Step through the door
at half past nine

Here is your cup
Here is your saucer

Sit in the yellow light
drinking hot black coffee

I CAN'T REMEMBER

I can't remember
you lifting me
from the tub

Surely you had to do those things

You were a shadow against the windows
against the faint light from the court

the shades rolled up completely
to use the light we had

You were a presence there and there

I was part of your motion
but not part of your skin

There was no softness

You moved
I watched my frog's leg
curve of belly
in the shallow water

disturbed the surface
tilted like a cup
over and over
hours and hours

sending against myself
the cool delicious transparency
hand open, hand closed

You were a spare resiliency
against the windows

Not softness of smooth skin, fingertip, cradling arm
or firm flushed cheek slipped against mine

not the full-eyed face of the sun
but your motion, your motion survives

MY FATHER WILL DIE WITHOUT WARNING

My father will die without warning
but he is dying slowly

Each morning
the day begins
What a wonder!

and the wave swells over me
the tidal mouth and shoulders

With my childish feet
with my strong legs
and my arms like a man

I dive in

Father
what do you take away
and what have you given?

When you sleep
your face is grey
and I listen at the door
for your breathing

Father, don't leave me
without warning

Can you find something to say?

But you are leaving already
you are leaving slowly without me

JOSEPH

Curled, head on hands, palm against palm,
like the Rebbe, you who were beardless
now hide the arrow of your bones,
who never told, dream and tell

Clearly   on First Street
in the pouring fall rain
in the first shock of cold
your dead mother comes toward you, and
you ask the simplest, saddest question
taking off your coat to cover her shoulders, and
she tells you what you know but do not yet believe
one hand in yours, and with the other
draws close the   wet   shining   coat

October 1975

87

THE STATION

In the high-ceilinged room
with the chandelier
we lay down to sleep with our father

not in the same bed
because there were no beds
and no goodnights

in fact, there were no words at all

Nothing we could bring
would be taken or eaten

we carried our hands

there were no drawers or shelves
not a ledge or a sill
or a hook or a bowl

not a chair or a table
or a sink or a toilet

Under the burning light
we lay down in our clothes
like refugees in a station

One by one we rose from sleep
and when we lifted the blue gauze
we saw the face of our father

He was smooth and calm as a baby
who would sleep the night
and would not cry or ask for anything

THE RAINBOW

Nature crept up—
hard tufts of green

Last night I dreamed
I was trying to skate
and had to learn again

The dull silver skates slipped
on over my oxfords
the key turned—

slippery glide on slate
cool as a blade on ice

the sky was a strip of grey
over the flat house-tops

sparse hedges for plucking
dirty river snaked past

Down   down
spin   around

small hands take hold
sweat grows in the grip

in and out of back alleys
bitter smell of weeds and piss

a tree twisted up in the crack

We called through the long night:
"All come home, come home."

The earth is pounded to iron
The rainbow spreads in oil

SENSE

What is more real
than fat white chickens
crowded in a pen

squawking
as you felt and chose

Hot blood sprung from their throats
dripping into fresh sawdust
the texture of oatmeal

the smell of burning feathers
was right as prayer
the sensate exactness of things:

carp swimming in a grey tank
lush fruit fermenting in a copper still

moist cavity of the fish
the yellow bursting sack
of eggs slick with slime

The bird is in the trees
The tanks are in the street
The South Vietnamese
are sweeping Tent City

Sick babies fly in, fly in

I am afraid of nostalgia
though I need to heal
What does a child know
except what she tastes and feels?

REMEMBER

Beside blue milk
and warm baths

remember how

Your arm trailed over
the side of the couch

You drifted in a boat
where I had laid you

The fire burned
always itself

its own meat
its own bone

I danced into my smile
holding your energy down

My bones sang like iron:

I could dance you into your grave!

Remember my face
in the light of the fire

How I turned and jumped into power

dancing, dancing you down

NIECE

I am my Aunt Rose
weaver of silk

Syphilitic daughter
of a syphilitic father
snow melted on your furs,
Rose of Paterson

I was the girl
who sat and waited

led your brother
to the blindmen's picnic
where seeing eye dogs
slept under the table

O to see when all are blind
to row the blind out in the pond

Niece
without a cane
without stiff buckram jacket

I belonged
and wasn't I favored and blessed?

Behind the green ordinary woods is a clearing
where blindmen are eating
with fine over-sensitive fingers

stiffly turning their heads toward me
threading the air between us

The mad women dance and wait
They do not know if it's night or day
They do not know if it's cold or hot

Taken inside the gate
but not behind the walls
fed from your basket
told and not told

I was drawn into the warp

Behind my mouth is the blindman's mouth
Behind my head is the rose

Across my feet
the dog is sleeping

I see   I see

How I am blessed

NOTES

Page 40, "Seeing Things." The phrase "the clangor of the Black Marias" is taken from Anna Akhmatova's long poem "Requiem" (*Poems of Akhmatova,* trans. Stanley Kunitz with Max Hayward, Boston: Little, Brown and Co., 1973).

Page 73, "Evidence." In her memoir, *Hope Against Hope* (New York: Atheneum, 1970), Nadezhda Mandelstam, the widow of the Russian poet Osip Mandelstam, describes how the textile workers of Strunino came to her window. Some left money on the sill for her escape.

This edition consists of one thousand copies, fifty of which have been numbered and signed by the author.

———————————

Designed by Frank R. DiFederico. Typeset by Mark S. Erickson. Printed by Universal Lithographers, Inc., Lutherville-Timonium, Md.